Lasting Legacy

Unleashing the Power of Seven Generations

Marquez Noodin

CopyRight

ISBN | 9798397070072

A Marquez Noodin Original

Table Of Contents

Introduction

Awakening the Wisdom of the Anishinaabe Teachings

Hi, my name is Misko Noodin (meaning Red Wind) also known as Marquez Noodin, an indigene of North America majoring in both History andMedieval Arts. I'll be writing this book in third person form(narrator) for better understanding. Sacred welcome.

In this powerful and transformative journey, we embark upon a sacred path—a path that leads us to the wisdom of the Anishinaabe teachings. As we open our hearts and minds, we awaken to the profound and timeless knowledge that has been passed down through generations.

The Anishinaabe, also known as the Ojibwe, Ojibway, or Chippewa, have a rich and extensive history. The origins of the Anishinaabe people can be traced back many centuries. According to oral traditions, the belief is that they have been living in the Great Lakes region of North America since time immemorial.

Archaeological evidence suggests that Anishinaabe ancestors have occupied parts of present-day Canada and the United States for thousands of years. They have maintained a deep connection to the land and have developed a unique culture, language, and way of life.

The Anishinaabe have a strong sense of their historical continuity, passing down their traditions, teachings, and stories through oral transmission from one generation to the next. Their history encompasses periods of migration, interactions with other Indigenous nations, and encounters with European settlers and colonization.

It is important to note that the Anishinaabe people are not a monolithic group but are made up of various distinct communities, each with its own unique history and experiences. They continue to thrive today, preserving their cultural heritage, participating in contemporary society, and advocating for their rights and sovereignty.

In the depths of our souls, we recognize the call to reconnect with the ancient wisdom that offers guidance, healing, and a profound sense of interconnectedness. It is an invitation to rediscover our place within the intricate web of life and honor the teachings that have sustained Indigenous communities for centuries.

Through this awakening, we begin to unravel the tapestry of the Anishinaabe philosophy—a philosophy rooted in harmony, respect, and love for all beings. It is a philosophy that teaches us to live in balance and unity with the natural world, recognizing that we are not separate from it but an integral part of its intricate fabric.

As we immerse ourselves in this journey, we embrace the teachings of the Seven Generations and the Seven Grandfathers—a sacred guidance system that offers profound insights into our purpose, relationships, and responsibilities as stewards of the Earth.

With reverence and humility, we explore the virtue of Nibwaakaawin—wisdom. It is through wisdom that we gain a deeper understanding of ourselves and the world around us. We learn to listen to the whispers of our ancestors, drawing upon their knowledge and experiences to navigate the complexities of modern life.

In the chapters that follow, we delve into each of the Seven Grandfathers' virtues—Zaagidwin (love), Mnaadendmowin (respect), Aakode'ewin (bravery),

Gwekwaadiziwin (honesty), Dbe'ewin (humility), and Debwewin (truth). We explore their significance, unravel their profound meaning, and uncover their transformative power in our lives.

Throughout this journey, we are reminded that these teachings are not confined to the pages of a book but are alive within us, waiting to be awakened. They call us to action, urging us to embody their wisdom and create positive change in our lives and the world around us.

As we embark upon this path of awakening, may our hearts be open, our spirits be receptive, and our intentions be pure. Together, let us honor the legacy of the Anishinaabe teachings, walking hand in hand with our ancestors and paving the way for future generations to come.

Welcome to this sacred journey of awakening—the journey to uncover the wisdom of the Anishinaabe teachings and create a world filled with love, respect, and interconnectedness.

Setting the Stage for Exploring the Profound Teachings of the Seven Generations and Seven Grandfathers.

Here we lay the foundation for our exploration of the profound teachings of the Seven Generations and Seven Grandfathers. We set the stage for a transformative journey that will take us deep into the heart of Indigenous wisdom and guide us towards a greater understanding of our place in the world.

We begin by acknowledging the immense richness and depth of Indigenous knowledge, recognizing that the teachings of the Seven Generations and Seven Grandfathers are not mere concepts but living, breathing truths that have sustained Indigenous communities for centuries. These teachings hold the wisdom of countless generations, passed down through storytelling, ceremony, and lived experiences.

As we embark on this journey, we invite you to set aside preconceived notions and open your heart to the profound teachings that await. We enter with a spirit of humility, recognizing that we are here to learn, to listen, and to honor the wisdom of the Anishinaabe people.

Together, we delve into the concept of the Seven Generations—an understanding that our actions today have consequences that ripple through time, affecting not only our present but also the lives of future generations. We come to grasp the immense responsibility we carry as stewards of the Earth and the importance of making choices that honor the well-being of all beings.

In parallel, we introduce the Seven Grandfathers, virtues that serve as guiding principles for living a harmonious and purposeful life. We explore the essence of each virtue—love, respect, bravery, honesty, humility, and truth—and contemplate their significance in our daily lives.

Throughout this chapter, we reflect on the interconnectedness of all things—the delicate balance that exists within the natural world and our role as caretakers of this precious planet. We contemplate the challenges we face in a rapidly changing world and recognize the urgency to reconnect with the timeless wisdom of the Anishinaabe teachings.

With reverence and gratitude, we honor the ancestral knowledge that has been entrusted to us. We acknowledge that this journey is not merely an intellectual exercise but a profound and transformative experience that has the potential to touch our hearts, awaken our spirits, and inspire meaningful change.

As we set the stage for the exploration of the Seven Generations and Seven Grandfathers, we invite you to embrace curiosity, to surrender to the wisdom that flows through these teachings, and to allow them to guide you on a path of personal growth, healing, and interconnectedness.

May this chapter serve as a doorway, opening us to the immense possibilities that await as we embark on this sacred journey of self-discovery and collective transformation. Let us step forward with reverence and embark on this extraordinary quest to unlock the power of the Seven Generations and Seven Grandfathers teachings.

CHAPTER 1

Anishinaabe Philosophy: A Path to Harmony and Interconnectedness

In this chapter, we embark on a profound journey into the heart of Anishinaabe philosophy—a philosophy deeply rooted in the wisdom of the Seven Generations and the teachings of the Seven Grandfathers. It is a path that beckons us to embrace harmony and interconnectedness, not only within ourselves but also with the world around us.

As we delve into the teachings of the Anishinaabe, we are invited to awaken our spirits and remember the sacredness of all life. We are reminded that we are not isolated beings but integral parts of a vast and intricate web of existence—a web where every action and every choice carries ripple effects that extend far beyond our immediate awareness.

The Anishinaabe philosophy emphasizes the interconnectedness of all things, urging us to recognize the profound relationships we share with nature, with our fellow human beings, and with the spiritual realms. It calls us to honor the sacredness of these relationships and to walk in unity with all beings, embracing a profound sense of respect, love, courage, truth, humility, and wisdom—the virtues embodied by the Seven Grandfathers.

Through this path, we learn to see ourselves as custodians of the Earth, entrusted with the responsibility to care for and protect the natural world. We discover the power of ceremony and ritual, which serve as bridges between the physical and spiritual realms, allowing us to commune with our ancestors, receive guidance, and express gratitude for the blessings bestowed upon us.

Moreover, Anishinaabe philosophy teaches us the importance of balance and wellness—of nurturing our physical, mental, emotional, and spiritual well-being. It guides us towards holistic healing practices, rooted in the wisdom of the land and the ancestral knowledge passed down through generations.

By embracing the path of Anishinaabe philosophy, we learn to live in alignment with the natural rhythms of life, cultivating a deep sense of harmony within ourselves and with the world. We come to understand that our individual actions have far-reaching consequences and that every choice we make can either contribute to the well-being of the Seven Generations to come or perpetuate a cycle of imbalance and disconnection.

In the chapters that follow, we will explore the various facets of Anishinaabe philosophy, delving deeper into the teachings of the Seven Generations and the Seven Grandfathers. We will uncover the significance of sacred ceremonies, the wisdom of healing practices, the importance of preserving cultural identity, and the role of indigenous rights advocacy in the pursuit of justice.

Prepare to embark on a transformative journey—one that will ignite your spirit, awaken your consciousness, and instill within you a profound appreciation for the interconnectedness of all life. Together, let us walk the path of Anishinaabe philosophy, embracing harmony, and weaving our threads into the tapestry of existence.

Delving into the Foundational Principles and Beliefs of the Anishinaabe People and their Teachings .

The Anishinaabe people, with their deep-rooted spiritual and cultural traditions, have long held profound wisdom that guides their way of life. By exploring their foundational principles and beliefs, we embark on a journey of understanding and appreciation for the teachings that have shaped their communities for generations.

At the heart of the Anishinaabe teachings lie the fundamental concepts of interconnectedness, balance, and harmony. These principles reflect a profound reverence for the natural world and the recognition that all living beings are interconnected and interdependent. The Anishinaabe people believe that every action has a ripple effect, affecting not only the present but also the well-being of future generations—the concept known as the Seven Generations.

Within the circle of life, the Anishinaabe honor the wisdom of their ancestors and embrace the responsibility to pass on this wisdom to future generations. They believe in the importance of maintaining a harmonious relationship with the land, water, plants, animals, and all beings that inhabit their territories. This deep respect for

Mother Earth and all her creations forms the foundation of their sustainable and balanced way of life.

Central to Anishinaabe teachings are the Seven Grandfathers, representing seven core virtues: love, respect, honesty, wisdom, humility, truth, and bravery. These virtues serve as guiding principles for individuals, families, and communities. By embodying these virtues, the Anishinaabe people strive to cultivate harmonious relationships, foster personal growth, and contribute to the well-being of the collective.

An essential aspect of Anishinaabe philosophy is the practice of ceremony and ritual. Ceremonies serve as powerful conduits for spiritual connection and guidance, providing opportunities to express gratitude, seek healing, and strengthen the bonds between individuals, communities, and the spiritual realm. Through ceremony, the Anishinaabe people honor their ancestors, seek harmony, and align themselves with the natural rhythms of the world.

The teachings of the Anishinaabe extend beyond individual well-being and touch upon broader issues of social and environmental justice. They advocate for the rights and sovereignty of indigenous peoples, recognizing the need to protect ancestral lands, preserve cultural heritage, and ensure the continuation of indigenous languages and traditions.

By delving into the foundational principles and beliefs of the Anishinaabe people, we gain profound insights into a way of life that honors interconnectedness, respects the wisdom of the past, and seeks to create a more balanced and harmonious world for future generations. Their teachings remind us of the importance of living in harmony with nature, fostering meaningful relationships, and embracing virtues that promote personal and communal flourishing.

As we explore these teachings, let us approach with an open heart and a willingness to learn from the wisdom of the Anishinaabe. Let us honor their legacy by incorporating their teachings into our own lives and communities, fostering a deeper understanding of our interconnectedness and nurturing a world that thrives on respect, love, and harmony.

CHAPTER 2

The Seven Generations: Embracing Intergenerational Responsibility

In a world where instant gratification and short-term thinking often prevail, the wisdom of the Seven Generations stands as a powerful reminder of our intergenerational responsibility. Rooted in indigenous teachings, this concept urges us to consider the impact of our actions not just on the present, but on the well-being and sustainability of future generations.

The philosophy of the Seven Generations teaches us to view time as an interconnected web, where the choices we make today reverberate through the lives of our children, grandchildren, and those yet to come. It invites us to expand our vision beyond immediate gains and think long-term, fostering a deep sense of stewardship for the Earth and all its inhabitants.

At its core, embracing intergenerational responsibility means recognizing that we are part of an ongoing narrative, woven together by the threads of past, present, and future. It calls us to honor the wisdom of our ancestors, draw strength from their experiences, and learn from their mistakes. Through this connection to our roots, we gain valuable insights that can inform our decisions and guide us towards a more sustainable and just future.

By embracing the teachings of the Seven Generations, we are prompted to consider the consequences of our actions on the natural world. We recognize that the resources we utilize today are not infinite, and that our choices regarding energy consumption, waste management, and environmental conservation have far-reaching implications. With this awareness, we can strive to adopt sustainable practices that preserve the integrity of our ecosystems and safeguard the planet for generations to come.

Intergenerational responsibility also extends to matters of social justice and equality. It calls us to confront and address systemic injustices that hinder the progress and well-being of future generations. By actively working towards dismantling inequalities, promoting inclusivity, and advocating for human rights, we pave the way for a more just society that can thrive for generations beyond our own.

Education plays a pivotal role in embodying the principles of intergenerational responsibility. By passing down knowledge, skills, and values to younger generations, we empower them to make informed choices, contribute meaningfully to society, and continue the cycle of learning and growth. Through mentorship, storytelling, and the preservation of cultural heritage, we foster a sense of identity, pride, and resilience that can uplift communities for generations to come.

Ultimately, embracing intergenerational responsibility is an act of love—a commitment to leave a positive and lasting legacy for those who will follow in our footsteps. It is a recognition of our interconnectedness and a deep-seated belief in the inherent worth and potential of every human being. By prioritizing the well-being of future generations, we transcend the boundaries of time and contribute to the collective flourishing of humanity.

As we embrace the teachings of the Seven Generations, let us reflect on the choices we make and the impact they have on our shared future. Let us embody the values of compassion, wisdom, and foresight, as we strive to create a world that honors its past, nurtures its present, and builds a better tomorrow. In doing so, we embark on a transformative journey of intergenerational responsibility—one that shapes not only our own lives but the legacy we leave behind for the generations to come.

Understanding the Concept of the Seven Generations and its Significance in Shaping our Actions and Decisions.

The concept of the Seven Generations holds profound wisdom and significance in guiding our actions and decisions. Rooted in indigenous teachings, it calls upon us to consider the long-term impact of our choices, not just for ourselves, but for the well-being of future generations. By understanding and embracing this concept, we gain a deeper appreciation for the interconnectedness of all life and the responsibility we have to leave a positive legacy.

At its core, the idea of the Seven Generations teaches us to think beyond the immediate present and to consider the consequences of our actions on the world around us. It invites us to become mindful stewards of the Earth and to think in terms of the impact our decisions will have on the seventh generation yet to come. This profound perspective challenges us to step away from short-term thinking and instead embrace a more holistic approach to life.

When we understand the concept of the Seven Generations, we recognize that our choices ripple outward, shaping the world not just for our own benefit, but for the well-being of our children, grandchildren, and beyond. This realization compels us to consider the long-term implications of our actions in various aspects of life, including environmental sustainability, social justice, and cultural preservation.

In terms of environmental sustainability, the concept of the Seven Generations emphasizes the importance of responsible resource management. We come to understand that the Earth's resources are finite and that our actions today can have a lasting impact on future generations. By adopting sustainable practices such as conservation, renewable energy, and responsible consumption, we contribute to the preservation of our planet and ensure that future generations will have access to a healthy and thriving environment.

The Seven Generations also guide our approach to social justice and equality. It reminds us of the interconnectedness of humanity and the importance of building a just and inclusive society. By addressing systemic injustices, promoting equality, and advocating for the rights of marginalized communities, we strive to create a world that is more equitable and compassionate, not just for ourselves, but for generations to come.

Cultural preservation is another significant aspect intertwined with the concept of the Seven Generations. It prompts us to honor and value our cultural heritage, recognizing that our traditions, languages, and practices are essential threads in the tapestry of humanity. By preserving and sharing our cultural wisdom with future generations, we ensure that our rich diversity and collective knowledge continue to thrive and inspire.

Understanding the concept of the Seven Generations challenges us to evaluate our choices through a broader lens—one that considers the long-term impact and intergenerational consequences. It compels us to ask ourselves, "How will this decision affect future generations? Will it contribute to their well-being and flourishing?"

By embodying the principles of the Seven Generations, we cultivate a profound sense of interconnectedness and responsibility. We recognize that our actions matter and that we have the power to shape a better world for future generations. This understanding ignites a sense of purpose and calls us to make choices aligned with the greater good, guided by wisdom, compassion, and a commitment to leaving a positive legacy.

In conclusion, the concept of the Seven Generations teaches us to think beyond ourselves and to consider the well-being of future generations in all aspects of life. It invites us to be mindful of the impact our choices have on the Earth, on society, and on our cultural heritage. By embracing this wisdom, we become agents of positive change, weaving a tapestry of intergenerational harmony and ensuring a brighter future for all.

CHAPTER 3

Nibwaakaawin - Wisdom: Illuminating the Path of Understanding

Wisdom is a timeless treasure that guides us on our journey through life, helping us navigate the complexities of the world with clarity and purpose. In the teachings of the Anishinaabe people, Nibwaakaawin represents the deep reservoir of ancestral knowledge and insight that illuminates our path toward understanding. It is through embracing this wisdom that we can connect with our true selves, our communities, and the interconnected web of life.

The essence of Nibwaakaawin lies in the profound understanding of the interdependence of all things. It teaches us to recognize the interconnectedness of nature, humanity, and the spiritual realm, fostering a sense of harmony and balance. This wisdom invites us to listen attentively to the whispers of the natural world, learning from its rhythms, cycles, and wisdom. By doing so, we gain a deeper appreciation for the interconnected web of life and our place within it.

At the heart of Nibwaakaawin is the understanding that wisdom is not solely acquired through individual experiences but is also passed down through generations. It recognizes the importance of learning from our ancestors, elders, and community, valuing their teachings as a source of wisdom and guidance. Through storytelling, ceremonies, and shared knowledge, the wisdom of the past is woven into the fabric of the present, enriching our lives and connecting us to the collective wisdom of our people.

In embracing Nibwaakaawin, we are invited to cultivate a deep sense of introspection and self-reflection. It encourages us to seek a profound understanding of our own purpose and place in the world. By connecting with our inner selves and embracing our unique gifts and strengths, we can contribute meaningfully to the greater whole. Nibwaakaawin teaches us to recognize that each of us carries a unique piece of the grand puzzle of existence, and by honoring and sharing our wisdom, we enrich the collective tapestry of humanity.

Wisdom is not confined to intellectual knowledge but encompasses a holistic understanding that integrates the mind, body, and spirit. Nibwaakaawin teaches us to listen to the whispers of our intuition, to honor the wisdom that resides within us, and to trust the guidance of our hearts. It invites us to cultivate mindfulness, presence, and deep respect for all beings, fostering a sense of reverence for life itself.

Through the illumination of Nibwaakaawin, we gain insight into the interconnectedness of all things and recognize our responsibility as stewards of the Earth. This wisdom calls us to walk gently upon the Earth, honoring and protecting the natural world. It reminds us that our actions ripple through the web of life, and our choices have the power to create a sustainable and harmonious future for all generations to come.

In conclusion, Nibwaakaawin - Wisdom is a guiding light that illuminates our path toward understanding. It invites us to recognize the interconnectedness of all things, to honor the wisdom of our ancestors, and to cultivate a deep sense of self-awareness and mindfulness. By embracing this wisdom, we connect with our true selves, our communities, and the world around us in a profound and meaningful way. Nibwaakaawin teaches us that wisdom is not merely intellectual knowledge, but a holistic understanding that integrates mind, body, and spirit. May we walk this path of wisdom with reverence and gratitude, enriching our lives and the lives of future generations.

Exploring the Virtue of Wisdom and its Role in Guiding our Thoughts, Choices, and Interactions with the World .

Wisdom, an ageless virtue cherished by humanity throughout the ages, holds a profound power to shape our lives and transform our perspectives. It serves as a guiding light, leading us toward deeper understanding, discernment, and harmony. In the tapestry of human virtues, wisdom stands tall as a beacon of insight, illuminating our path and influencing our thoughts, choices, and interactions with the world.

The Anishinaabe teachings, rooted in the wisdom of the Seven Generations and the guidance of the

Seven Grandfathers, offer us a rich tapestry of wisdom that transcends time and culture. It invites us to explore the essence of wisdom and its vital role in our lives. By delving into these teachings, we embark on a journey of self-discovery and enlightenment, unraveling the layers of our consciousness and expanding our awareness of the world around us.

Wisdom, at its core, encompasses more than mere knowledge or intelligence. It is a holistic virtue that integrates intellect, intuition, and spiritual insight. It embraces the deep understanding of the interconnectedness of all things and encourages us to see beyond the surface, to recognize the hidden patterns and underlying truths that shape our existence. Wisdom compels us to delve into the depths of our hearts and minds, seeking clarity and guidance as we navigate the complexities of life.

Through the teachings of the Anishinaabe, we learn that wisdom is not a solitary pursuit but a shared endeavor. It is through collective experiences, intergenerational knowledge, and the wisdom of our elders and ancestors that we gain a broader perspective. Wisdom invites us to engage in deep listening, to honor the stories and teachings passed down from generation to generation. By embracing this communal wisdom, we tap into a reservoir of insights and perspectives that enrich our own understanding.

Wisdom plays a pivotal role in guiding our thoughts, choices, and interactions with the world. It empowers us to make informed decisions, to see beyond immediate gratification, and to consider the long-term consequences of our actions. It urges us to reflect on the interconnectedness of our choices, recognizing that each decision we make has a ripple effect on ourselves, our communities, and the natural world. Wisdom calls us to be mindful of our impact and to strive for actions that align with the greater good.

Furthermore, wisdom invites us to cultivate a deep sense of empathy and compassion, fostering harmonious relationships and nurturing a sense of interconnectedness. It teaches us to listen with an open heart, to embrace diverse perspectives, and to approach conflicts with patience and understanding. By infusing our interactions with wisdom, we create spaces for growth, healing, and collaboration, fostering a sense of unity and harmony in our communities.

In conclusion, the exploration of the virtue of wisdom is an enriching and transformative journey. It invites us to dive deep into our own consciousness, to seek the wisdom of our ancestors, and to engage in a lifelong quest for understanding. The teachings of the Anishinaabe, rooted in the wisdom of the Seven Generations and the Seven

Grandfathers, offer us profound insights into the essence of wisdom and its role in shaping our thoughts, choices, and interactions with the world. May we embrace wisdom as a guiding force in our lives, walking the path of enlightenment and contributing to a more harmonious and compassionate world for all.

CHAPTER 4

Zaagi'idiwin - Love: Cultivating Compassion and Unity

Love, a universal force that transcends boundaries and touches the deepest corners of our hearts, has the power to transform lives and shape the world we inhabit. It is a timeless virtue that weaves together the threads of compassion, empathy, and unity, connecting us to one another and to the greater tapestry of existence. In the teachings of the Anishinaabe, the concept of Zaagidwin - love - holds a sacred place, inviting us to delve into its essence and cultivate its profound qualities within ourselves and within our communities.

At its essence, Zaagidwin is not merely a fleeting emotion or a romantic notion. It is a boundless force that emanates from the core of our being, embracing all living beings and extending beyond the boundaries of time and space. It calls us to cultivate compassion, kindness, and understanding in our interactions with others, fostering unity and harmony in our relationships.

The teachings of the Anishinaabe guide us to recognize that love begins with self-love. By nurturing a deep sense of love and acceptance for ourselves, we are better equipped to extend that love outward, radiating its transformative energy to those around us. Zaagidwin teaches us that love is not conditional but all-encompassing, embracing the beauty and imperfections of every individual. It encourages us to see the interconnectedness of all beings and to honor the inherent worth and dignity of each person we encounter.

Love, in its purest form, fosters empathy and understanding. It invites us to listen with an open heart, to truly see and hear the experiences and perspectives of others. Through the practice of active compassion, we can bridge divides, dissolve barriers, and foster unity. Zaagidwin reminds us that we are all interconnected, and by embracing love, we can create a world that values inclusivity, justice, and equality.

Moreover, love challenges us to act with integrity and to stand in solidarity with those who face injustice and adversity. It compels us to confront systems of oppression, discrimination, and violence, advocating for a world where every individual can thrive. Zaagidwin reminds us that love is not passive but a catalyst for change, empowering us to be agents of compassion and justice in our communities.

In cultivating Zaagidwin, we embark on a transformative journey of self-discovery and growth. It requires us to let go of ego-driven desires and embrace a mindset of humility and interconnectedness. Love invites us to set aside judgment, to embrace forgiveness and reconciliation, and to extend grace to ourselves and others. It encourages us to celebrate diversity and to recognize the inherent value of every culture, belief system, and way of life.

As we embrace the teachings of Zaagidwin, we contribute to the creation of a more compassionate and harmonious world. Love has the power to heal wounds, mend broken relationships, and bring communities together. It serves as a guiding light, illuminating our path and inspiring us to create a world where love is the driving force behind our actions, decisions, and interactions.

In conclusion, Zaagidwin - love - holds a sacred place in the teachings of the Anishinaabe. It is a virtue that transcends boundaries and speaks to the core of our humanity. By cultivating compassion, empathy, and unity, we can embrace the transformative power of love and contribute to a world where every individual is seen, valued, and cherished. May Zaagidwin guide us in our journey toward unity, compassion, and a more loving world for all.

Examining the Power of Love as a Transformative Force for Fostering Connections and Creating Harmonious Relationships.

Love, a force that transcends time and space, has the extraordinary power to transform lives, foster deep connections, and create harmonious relationships. It is a force that knows no boundaries, defies logic, and has the ability to bring about profound change in our world. In the teachings of the Anishinaabe, love holds a sacred place, offering wisdom and guidance on how we can harness its transformative potential to cultivate meaningful connections and create harmonious relationships.

Love, at its core, is a universal language that speaks to the depths of our souls. It is a force that calls us to recognize the inherent worth and value of every individual, and to treat one another with kindness, compassion, and respect. In the Anishinaabe tradition, love is seen as an interconnected web that binds us all together, reminding us of our shared humanity and the importance of nurturing relationships based on love and understanding.

When we open our hearts to love, we create a fertile ground for connections to flourish. Love allows us to see beyond differences, to embrace diversity, and to appreciate the unique gifts and contributions that each person brings to the tapestry of life. It invites us to listen deeply, to empathize with one another's joys and sorrows, and to create spaces where everyone feels seen, heard, and valued.

The transformative power of love lies not only in its ability to connect individuals but also in its capacity to heal and mend broken relationships. Love teaches us forgiveness, understanding, and the art of letting go. It invites us to release grudges, resentments, and judgments, and to approach relationships with an open heart and a willingness to reconcile. In the Anishinaabe teachings, love is viewed as a sacred responsibility that requires us to work through conflicts, find common ground, and restore balance and harmony in our interactions.

Love is also a force that empowers us to extend kindness and compassion to ourselves. By practicing self-love and self-care, we cultivate a deep sense of worthiness and nurture our own well-being. When we fill our own cup with love, we have more to offer to others, and our relationships become grounded in authenticity, vulnerability, and genuine care.

In a world that often seems divided and disconnected, the power of love becomes even more essential. It serves as a beacon of hope, reminding us of our shared humanity and the innate capacity we possess to create positive change. Love inspires acts of kindness, generosity, and selflessness, encouraging us to reach out to those in need and to stand in solidarity with one another. It has the power to transcend barriers, bridge divides, and create a world where compassion, understanding, and love are the guiding principles.

As we examine the power of love, we are called to reflect on our own relationships and interactions. Are we nurturing love in our connections? Are we approaching others with kindness, compassion, and empathy? Are we cultivating harmonious relationships that honor the principles of love and understanding?

In conclusion, love is a transformative force that has the potential to foster deep connections, heal wounds, and create harmonious relationships. It is a force that unites us, inspires us, and guides us in our quest for a more compassionate and loving world. By embracing love in all its forms, we have the power to transform ourselves, our relationships, and ultimately, the world around us. May we recognize the immense power of love and cultivate its presence in our lives, allowing it to guide us on a journey of connection, understanding, and harmonious relationships.

CHAPTER 5

Mnaadendmowin - Respect: Honoring the Interconnectedness of All Beings

In the teachings of the Anishinaabe people, Mnaadendmowin, or respect, holds a sacred place as a guiding principle in how we interact with the world around us. It is a virtue that encompasses a deep appreciation for the interconnectedness of all beings and emphasizes the value and worthiness of each individual and entity. Mnaadendmowin teaches us to honor and uphold this interconnected web of life, fostering a harmonious and balanced existence for ourselves, others, and the natural world.

At the heart of Mnaadendmowin lies the recognition that everything in the universe is connected. We are all part of a grand tapestry, woven together by invisible threads that bind us to one another and to the Earth. With this understanding, we approach life with humility, recognizing that each being, whether human, animal, or plant, has its own unique purpose and contribution to make.

Respect begins with honoring ourselves. It is about embracing our own inherent worth and treating ourselves with kindness, compassion, and acceptance. When we respect ourselves, we cultivate a healthy sense of self-esteem and well-being, which in turn allows us to extend that respect to others. By nurturing our own physical, emotional, and spiritual needs, we create a solid foundation from which respect can flow outward.

Mnaadendmowin also calls upon us to honor others. It invites us to see beyond differences and appreciate the diverse tapestry of humanity. Respect requires us to listen deeply, to seek understanding, and to value the experiences and perspectives of others. It is through this act of deep listening and empathy that bridges are built, relationships are strengthened, and communities flourish.

Respecting the natural world is a fundamental aspect of Mnaadendmowin. It acknowledges the sacredness of the Earth and our responsibility as stewards of its resources. When we respect the natural world, we recognize the interdependence between all living beings and the delicate balance that sustains life. We strive to live in harmony with nature, treating it with reverence, and seeking to minimize our impact on its delicate ecosystems.

By embracing Mnaadendmowin, we invite a profound shift in our consciousness. We begin to see ourselves as part of a larger whole, intimately connected to the web of life. This shift opens our hearts to the beauty and wisdom that exists in every being and instills a sense of gratitude for the gifts that surround us.

Practicing Mnaadendmowin requires conscious intention and daily commitment. It involves embodying values such as kindness, empathy, and compassion in our interactions with others. It entails nurturing a deep reverence for the Earth and making choices that reflect our interconnectedness with the natural world.

As we embrace Mnaadendmowin, we honor the interconnectedness of all beings. We come to understand that our actions have ripple effects that extend far beyond ourselves. By embodying respect in our thoughts, words, and deeds, we contribute to the creation of a world that is rooted in harmony, compassion, and balance.

In conclusion, Mnaadendmowin teaches us the importance of respect in honoring the interconnectedness of all beings. It invites us to see ourselves, others, and the natural world through the lens of reverence and appreciation. Through respect, we create a harmonious and balanced existence, where all beings are valued, heard, and cherished. Let us walk this path of respect, embracing the teachings of Mnaadendmowin, and nurturing a world that celebrates the interconnectedness and worthiness of all.

Understanding the Importance of Respect for Oneself, Others, and the Natural World, and its Role in Maintaining Balance and Harmony.

Respect, a fundamental principle deeply rooted in the teachings of the Anishinaabe people, holds immense significance in maintaining balance and harmony within ourselves, our relationships, and the natural world. It is an essential virtue that guides our actions, shapes our perspectives, and fosters a deep sense of interconnectedness.

At its core, respect begins with honoring oneself. It calls us to recognize our own worth, embrace our unique strengths and talents, and nurture a healthy sense of self-esteem. When we respect ourselves, we create a solid foundation for growth, self-care, and personal development. We acknowledge our inherent value as human beings and treat ourselves with kindness, compassion, and forgiveness.

Respecting others is equally vital in maintaining harmonious relationships. It requires us to embrace diversity, appreciate different perspectives, and cultivate empathy and understanding. By valuing the inherent worth of every individual, we create spaces of inclusivity, where everyone feels seen, heard, and respected. Through respectful interactions, we build bridges of connection, foster collaboration, and nurture a sense of community.

Respect extends beyond human relationships and encompasses our connection with the natural world. The Anishinaabe teachings emphasize the sacredness of the Earth and the interdependence between all living beings. By respecting the natural world, we acknowledge our responsibility as caretakers and stewards of the Earth. We strive to live in harmony with nature, honoring its cycles, protecting its resources, and preserving its beauty for future generations.

Respect for oneself, others, and the natural world intertwines to create a delicate balance. When we respect ourselves, we are better equipped to extend respect to others, and vice versa. This interconnected web of respect forms the foundation for healthy relationships, strong communities, and a sustainable relationship with the Earth.

Maintaining balance and harmony requires a commitment to respect in all aspects of life. It calls for conscious actions and choices that align with the principles of respect. This includes active listening, valuing diverse perspectives, practicing empathy, resolving conflicts peacefully, and demonstrating gratitude for the gifts of the natural world.

When we prioritize respect, we contribute to the well-being of ourselves, others, and the Earth. Respect fosters a sense of belonging, acceptance, and safety. It creates an environment where individuals can thrive, where conflicts can be resolved, and where cooperation and collaboration can flourish. By treating ourselves, others, and the natural world with respect, we contribute to the greater tapestry of life and promote a harmonious and sustainable future.

In conclusion, understanding the importance of respect for oneself, others, and the natural world is essential in maintaining balance and harmony. It is a guiding principle that encourages us to honor our own worth, embrace diversity, and cultivate a deep sense of interconnectedness. By living with respect as our compass, we foster healthy relationships, build vibrant communities, and forge a harmonious relationship with the Earth. Let us embrace respect as a transformative force in our lives, allowing it to guide our actions and shape a more balanced and harmonious world for generations to come.

CHAPTER 6

Aakode'ewin - Bravery: Embracing Courage in the Face of Challenges

In the journey of life, we often encounter obstacles and trials that test our resolve and push us beyond our comfort zones. It is during these moments that the virtue of Aakode'ewin, or bravery, emerges as a guiding force, urging us to embrace courage and face our challenges head-on. Aakode'ewin teaches us the importance of summoning our inner strength, finding resilience in adversity, and daring to step into the unknown.

Bravery is not the absence of fear but rather the ability to act despite it. It is a state of mind that empowers us to confront our fears and uncertainties, to stand firm in the face of adversity, and to take bold and decisive action. Aakode'ewin reminds us that growth and transformation often require us to venture outside our comfort zones and embrace the unknown with open hearts and minds.

One of the core aspects of Aakode'ewin is the willingness to face our fears and embrace discomfort. It encourages us to push past our self-imposed limitations and explore new territories. By doing so, we expand our horizons, discover hidden strengths, and unleash our true potential. Bravery invites us to step into the realm of possibility, where growth and personal development flourish.

At the heart of Aakode'ewin lies the recognition that true courage is not a solitary endeavor. It is intertwined with the support and encouragement of others. Just as the Anishinaabe people draw strength from their community, we too can seek solace and inspiration from our relationships. Together, we can navigate the uncertain paths of life, offering each other comfort, guidance, and unwavering support.

Aakode'ewin teaches us to find courage in the stories of our ancestors, who faced immense challenges and triumphed through their bravery. By embracing their wisdom and drawing from their experiences, we tap into a reservoir of strength that fuels our own bravery. Their stories remind us that we are part of a larger narrative, carrying the torch of courage that has been passed down through generations.

Embracing Aakode'ewin is a transformative journey that requires perseverance, self-belief, and a deep connection to our innermost selves. It calls us to challenge the status quo, to question limiting beliefs, and to forge our own paths with unwavering determination. Through bravery, we open ourselves to new opportunities, experiences, and perspectives, enriching our lives in ways we never thought possible.

In our modern world, Aakode'ewin holds profound relevance. It encourages us to confront the pressing issues of our time, to stand up for justice, and to advocate for positive change. Bravery empowers us to speak our truths, to challenge societal norms, and to champion the causes that align with our values. It is through acts of bravery, both big and small, that we contribute to a more just, equitable, and compassionate world.

As we embark on the path of Aakode'ewin, let us remember that bravery is not an elusive trait reserved for a select few. It is a quality that resides within each of us, waiting to be awakened and nurtured. By cultivating bravery in our lives, we inspire others to do the same, creating a ripple effect of courage and transformation.

In conclusion, Aakode'ewin teaches us to embrace courage in the face of challenges. It calls upon us to confront our fears, step into the unknown, and tap into our inner reservoir of strength. Through bravery, we expand our horizons, inspire others, and contribute to the betterment of our world. Let us walk the path of Aakode'ewin, knowing that within us lies the power to overcome

Exploring the Virtue of Bravery and How it Empowers us to Overcome Fear, Adversity, and Self-limiting Beliefs .

In the depths of our souls, there exists a flame of courage that can illuminate the darkest corners of our lives. This flame is the essence of bravery, a virtue that empowers us to face our fears, conquer adversity, and break free from the shackles of self-limiting beliefs. Bravery is not the absence of fear, but rather the willingness to confront it head-on and move forward with unwavering determination.

At the core of bravery lies the understanding that fear is a natural part of the human experience. It is an emotion that can either paralyze us or propel us forward. When we choose bravery, we acknowledge our fears but refuse to let them dictate our actions. We step into the unknown, fully aware of the risks, yet driven by a deep desire for growth and transformation.

Bravery encourages us to embrace discomfort and uncertainty, for it is within these realms that true personal development flourishes. It invites us to step outside the boundaries of our comfort zones and explore uncharted territories. In doing so, we discover hidden reservoirs of strength and resilience that we never knew existed.

Adversity is an inevitable part of life, but it is through acts of bravery that we rise above its challenges. Bravery grants us the fortitude to persevere when faced with obstacles, setbacks, and failures. It compels us to view adversity as an opportunity for growth and learning, rather than a roadblock to our dreams.

One of the most powerful aspects of bravery is its ability to shatter self-limiting beliefs. It nudges us to question the narratives we have constructed about ourselves and our abilities. Bravery empowers us to challenge the notion that we are not capable, deserving, or worthy of pursuing our dreams. It whispers in our ear, urging us to take that first step towards greatness, even when doubt threatens to hold us back.

Through acts of bravery, we redefine the boundaries of what is possible. We venture into uncharted territories, both in our external world and within ourselves. Bravery encourages us to face our insecurities, embrace vulnerability, and let go of the limitations that hinder our growth. It allows us to unleash our full potential and step into the greatness that resides within us.

But bravery is not a solitary endeavor. It thrives in the presence of support, encouragement, and camaraderie. When we surround ourselves with like-minded individuals who embody bravery, their courage becomes contagious. We draw strength from their stories, their triumphs, and their unwavering belief in themselves. Together, we create a community that fosters bravery and inspires others to embark on their own courageous journeys.

To cultivate bravery, we must nurture a mindset that embraces resilience, determination, and self-belief. We must silence the inner critic that whispers doubts and insecurities, and instead, listen to the voice of bravery that encourages us to take risks and seize opportunities. Bravery requires us to become the hero of our own story, to be willing to face our fears and overcome the obstacles that stand in our way.

In conclusion, bravery is a virtue that empowers us to overcome fear, adversity, and self-limiting beliefs. It is a flame within us that can be ignited through conscious choice and intentional action. By embracing bravery, we embark on a transformative journey of personal growth, unlocking our true potential and becoming the heroes of our own lives. So, let us embrace bravery and dare to live boldly, for it is through acts of bravery that we create a life of fulfillment, purpose, and true empowerment.

CHAPTER 7

Gwekwaadiziwin - Honesty: Living in Truth and Authenticity

In a world where facades and pretenses often prevail, the virtue of honesty stands as a beacon of light, guiding us back to our truest selves. Gwekwaadiziwin, the Anishinaabe concept of honesty, invites us to embrace a life of truth and authenticity, both in our words and our actions. It calls upon us to be genuine, transparent, and accountable in all aspects of our lives.

At its core, honesty is more than simply telling the truth. It is a way of being that requires us to align our thoughts, intentions, and behaviors with our deepest values and beliefs. It is a commitment to live in integrity, even when faced with difficult choices or uncomfortable circumstances.

Gwekwaadiziwin compels us to examine our motives and intentions, encouraging us to be honest with ourselves first and foremost. It invites us to confront our own fears, insecurities, and shortcomings, and to embrace vulnerability as a means of growth and connection. By being honest with ourselves, we pave the way for authentic relationships, genuine interactions, and a profound sense of inner peace.

Living in truth and authenticity requires the courage to express our thoughts and feelings openly and honestly, while also respecting the perspectives of others. It means being truthful in our communication, both with ourselves and with those around us. Honesty builds trust, fosters understanding, and creates a foundation for meaningful connections and relationships.

Gwekwaadiziwin challenges us to examine the stories we tell ourselves and others, questioning the narratives that may be rooted in falsehoods or self-deception. It invites us to shed the masks we wear, to let go of the need for approval or validation, and to embrace the liberation that comes with living authentically.

Honesty also extends beyond our individual lives and encompasses our relationship with the natural world. It calls us to be honest stewards of the Earth, recognizing our interconnectedness and the responsibility we bear for its well-being. By living in harmony with nature and honoring its resources, we demonstrate our commitment to honesty and respect for the web of life.

In a world often plagued by deception, dishonesty, and manipulation, embracing gwekwaadiziwin becomes a radical act of reclaiming our personal power and contributing to the collective well-being. It requires us to be brave, vulnerable, and accountable for our words and actions. By embodying honesty, we create an environment of trust, authenticity, and genuine connection, not only within ourselves but also in our interactions with others.

Living in truth and authenticity is not always easy. It demands self-reflection, self-awareness, and a willingness to confront uncomfortable truths. It challenges us to let go of societal expectations, to embrace vulnerability, and to be unapologetically ourselves. Yet, the rewards are immeasurable: a life lived with integrity, a sense of inner peace, and meaningful connections that arise from genuine interactions.

In conclusion, gwekwaadiziwin, the virtue of honesty, is a powerful guiding principle that invites us to live in truth and authenticity. It empowers us to be genuine, transparent, and accountable in our thoughts, words, and actions. By embracing gwekwaadiziwin, we cultivate trust, foster meaningful connections, and create a more harmonious and authentic life. Let us embark on this transformative journey of honesty and allow its light to illuminate our path towards personal growth, fulfillment, and a deeper sense of purpose.

Reflecting on the Power of Honesty as a Guiding Principle for Living a Genuine and Purposeful Life.

Honesty, both with ourselves and with others, is a transformative force that enables us to navigate our journey with clarity, integrity, and a deep sense of fulfillment.

Honesty is about embracing truth in all aspects of our lives. It starts with being honest with ourselves – acknowledging our strengths, weaknesses, fears, and aspirations. By facing our inner truths, we unlock the door to self-awareness and self-acceptance. We gain a clearer understanding of who we are, what truly matters to us, and the path we wish to walk.

Living a genuine life requires the courage to be honest with others as well. Authentic connections are forged through open and transparent communication. When we share our thoughts, feelings, and experiences truthfully, we invite others into our world and create a space for genuine connection and understanding. Honesty builds trust and cultivates relationships that are built on a solid foundation.

One of the most powerful aspects of honesty is its ability to align our actions with our values and beliefs. When we make choices that are grounded in honesty, we live in congruence with our authentic selves. This alignment brings a sense of harmony and peace, as we no longer feel the burden of wearing masks or pretending to be someone we're not. Honesty liberates us from the shackles of pretense, allowing us to express our true essence and contribute to the world in a meaningful way.

Living a purposeful life is intimately tied to honesty. When we are honest with ourselves, we gain clarity about our passions, dreams, and goals. We recognize the values that guide us and the impact we wish to make. Honesty becomes a compass that helps us navigate the choices and decisions that align with our purpose. It empowers us to make choices that are in line with our values, even when they may be challenging or require us to step outside our comfort zone.

Honesty also invites us to practice self-reflection and introspection. By honestly examining our thoughts, actions, and patterns, we open ourselves up to growth and transformation. We become aware of areas where we can improve, evolve, and align more deeply with our true selves. Honest self-reflection allows us to break free from self-limiting beliefs and embrace our fullest potential.

In a world that sometimes values deception and hidden agendas, embracing the power of honesty can feel like a revolutionary act. It requires vulnerability, courage, and a commitment to personal integrity. Yet, the rewards are immeasurable. When we choose honesty, we foster deeper connections, nurture authentic relationships, and create a ripple effect of trust and authenticity in our communities.

So, let us take a moment to reflect on the power of honesty as a guiding principle for living a genuine and purposeful life. Let us embrace the truth within ourselves and courageously share it with others. Through honesty, we embark on a journey of self-discovery, connection, and personal growth. We unlock the door to living a life of authenticity, fulfillment, and profound meaning. May we be guided by the power of honesty as we navigate our paths and contribute to a world that values truth, integrity, and genuine connection.

CHAPTER 8

Dabaadendiziwin - Humility: Embracing Humility as a Source of Strength

In a world that often celebrates self-promotion and individual accomplishments, the virtue of humility also stands as a beacon of light, reminding us of the transformative power found in embracing modesty, gratitude, and a deep understanding of our place in the greater tapestry of life. Dbe'ewin, the Anishinaabe teaching of humility, invites us to recognize that true strength lies not in asserting dominance or seeking recognition, but in our ability to cultivate a genuine sense of humility and honor the interconnectedness of all beings.

Humility is not about diminishing ourselves or downplaying our achievements. It is an acknowledgement of our inherent limitations, a recognition that we are part of something greater than ourselves. It is a virtue that encourages us to listen, to learn from others, and to approach life with an open mind and heart. Humility allows us to set aside our ego-driven desires for validation and instead focus on fostering harmony and cooperation within our communities and the natural world.

When we embrace humility, we open ourselves to the wisdom and teachings of others. We acknowledge that no single person holds all the answers, and that true growth comes from a collective sharing of knowledge and experiences. Humility invites us to be receptive to feedback, to learn from our mistakes, and to continuously strive for personal and spiritual growth. It is a humbling reminder that we are always works in progress, forever evolving and learning from the world around us.

Humility also fosters a deep sense of gratitude. When we approach life with humility, we recognize the countless blessings and gifts that come our way. We appreciate the interconnected web of relationships that support us, the beauty of the natural world, and the opportunities that present themselves. Gratitude, born from humility, enables us to cultivate a mindset of abundance and contentment, even in the face of challenges. It allows us to find joy in the simple moments, to appreciate the contributions of others, and to live with a spirit of generosity and compassion.

In a society that often values individual achievements and self-centered pursuits, embracing humility may seem counterintuitive. However, it is through humility that we find true strength. Humility empowers us to release the need for control, to let go of our attachments to outcomes, and to surrender to the natural flow of life. It encourages us to celebrate the successes and strengths of others, recognizing that their achievements do not diminish our own. Instead, it inspires us to uplift and support one another, to create a collective energy of empowerment and growth.

By embracing humility, we become agents of positive change in our communities and the world. We lead with compassion, empathy, and a deep respect for the interconnectedness of all beings. Humility fosters a sense of unity, dismantling the barriers that divide us and allowing us to work together towards common goals. It teaches us to value collaboration over competition and to approach challenges with grace and understanding.

Let us reflect on the wisdom of Dbe'ewin, the teaching of humility, and its significance in our lives. May we embody humility as a source of strength, allowing it to guide our actions, decisions, and interactions with others. In doing so, we honor the interconnectedness of all beings, foster genuine connections, and contribute to a world rooted in harmony, respect, and collective well-being.

Examining the Virtue of Humility and its Role in Fostering Personal Growth, Empathy, and Respectful Interactions.

Embracing the essence of humility can be a transformative journey that opens our hearts and minds to profound growth and understanding. In a society that often celebrates achievement and self-promotion, the virtue of humility stands as a beacon of light, reminding us of the power that lies in acknowledging our own limitations and recognizing the inherent worth of others. It is through the practice of humility that we cultivate empathy, foster meaningful connections, and create a world rooted in respect and harmony.

At its core, humility is not a sign of weakness or inferiority but a profound strength that allows us to transcend our ego-driven desires and embrace a greater perspective. It is the recognition that we are all interconnected, part of a vast tapestry of humanity. Humility urges us to let go of our need for validation and status, inviting us to appreciate the beauty and wisdom that exists in every individual we encounter.

When we embody humility, we become open to learning from others, valuing their insights and experiences. It is in these moments of humility that our own knowledge expands, our minds enriched by the wisdom of those around us. By recognizing that we don't have all the answers, we invite the opportunity for growth and transformation, allowing ourselves to evolve into better versions of ourselves.

Moreover, humility enables us to embrace the power of empathy—the ability to step into another person's shoes, understand their struggles, and offer compassion. Through humility, we shed the barriers of judgment and self-centeredness, creating a safe space for others to express themselves authentically. By listening deeply and acknowledging the validity of their experiences, we foster an environment of trust and connection, building bridges that unite us rather than walls that divide us.

In a world often characterized by rivalry and competition, humility reminds us that true success lies not in outshining others but in contributing to the greater good. It encourages us to celebrate the accomplishments of others, offering genuine support and encouragement. In doing so, we cultivate a culture of collaboration and cooperation, where the collective triumphs are cherished above individual victories.

Practicing humility requires inner reflection and a commitment to continuous self-improvement. It calls upon us to acknowledge our mistakes, take responsibility for our actions, and seek forgiveness when necessary. By embracing humility, we break free from the chains of ego and allow ourselves to evolve into more compassionate, understanding beings.

In our interactions with the natural world, humility prompts us to recognize our place within the intricate web of life. It reminds us to tread gently, honoring the Earth's resources and cherishing the delicate balance that sustains us. By cultivating a deep reverence for nature, we foster a sense of interconnectedness and inspire stewardship, becoming advocates for environmental preservation and sustainable practices.

In conclusion, the virtue of humility holds profound transformative power. It guides us towards personal growth, empathy, and respectful interactions. By embracing humility, we tap into our inner strength, expand our capacity for understanding, and foster harmonious relationships with others and the world around us. Let us walk this path with grace and humility, knowing that true greatness lies not in grandiosity but in the sincere embrace of our shared humanity.

CHAPTER 9

Debwewin - Truth: Seeking and Embracing Truth in All Aspects of Life

The virtue of truth, known as Debwewin in Anishinaabe teachings, is a powerful force that beckons us to seek and embrace its essence in every facet of our lives. Debwewin guides us to live with honesty, authenticity, and integrity, offering a path to navigate the complexities of existence and foster genuine connections with ourselves, others, and the world around us.

At its core, Debwewin invites us to examine our beliefs, question societal narratives, and embark on a journey of self-discovery. It encourages us to delve deep into our values, confront our fears, and challenge our biases. By embracing truth, we uncover our authentic selves, shedding societal masks that hinder our growth and hinder our ability to live in alignment with our deepest values.

The pursuit of truth requires open-mindedness and intellectual curiosity. It compels us to critically evaluate information, discerning between what is genuine and what is misleading. In a world where misinformation runs rampant, it is our responsibility to navigate through the noise, developing a discerning eye for truth. By doing so, we equip ourselves with the tools necessary to make informed decisions and contribute positively to our communities.

Embracing truth also calls for acknowledging and addressing uncomfortable realities. It demands courage to face the shadows within ourselves and society, to confront systemic injustices, and to work towards healing and transformation. By shining a light on these truths, we pave the way for positive change and strive towards a more just and equitable world.

Truth forms the foundation for authentic and meaningful relationships. When we approach interactions with honesty and transparency, we foster trust and create spaces where vulnerability and genuine connection thrive. By speaking our truths and listening with empathy and compassion, we honor the dignity and worth of others, building bridges of understanding and empathy.

In our relationship with the natural world, Debwewin urges us to recognize our interconnectedness and embrace our role as Earth's stewards. It compels us to acknowledge the truth of our impact on the environment and make conscious choices that promote sustainability and ecological balance. By aligning our actions with the truth of our interconnectedness, we contribute to the well-being of future generations and the preservation of our planet.

Living a life rooted in Debwewin requires ongoing reflection and a commitment to personal growth. It necessitates humility and the willingness to acknowledge when we have strayed from the path of truth. It calls upon us to learn from our mistakes, seek reconciliation, and make amends when necessary. By embracing Debwewin, we cultivate authenticity, integrity, and a deep sense of alignment with our values.

In conclusion, Debwewin, the Anishinaabe concept of truth, holds immense power in guiding our lives. By seeking and embracing truth in all aspects of our existence, we embark on a transformative journey of self-discovery, build meaningful relationships, and contribute to the well-being of our communities and the natural world. Let us embrace Debwewin with courage and integrity, knowing that in the pursuit of truth, we unlock the potential for personal growth, social harmony, and a more authentic and purposeful life.

Exploring the Concept of Truth and the Importance of Seeking Knowledge, Understanding, and Inner Alignment.

Truth, a concept deeply embedded in the fabric of human existence, beckons us to embark on a profound journey of exploration and self-discovery. It is a guiding light that illuminates our path, urging us to seek knowledge, understanding, and inner alignment. In a world where misinformation and half-truths abound, the pursuit of truth becomes an indispensable compass for navigating the complexities of life.

At its essence, truth transcends mere facts and figures. It encompasses a deeper understanding of the world and our place within it. It encompasses a harmony between our external experiences and our internal wisdom. Seeking truth is not merely an intellectual exercise but a deeply spiritual and transformative process that invites us to question, reflect, and delve into the depths of our being.

To embark on the journey of truth-seeking is to embrace the power of knowledge. It is an acknowledgement that true wisdom lies not in blind acceptance, but in the continuous pursuit of understanding. By seeking knowledge through various sources, we expand our horizons, challenge preconceived notions, and gain a broader perspective. The pursuit of truth demands an open mind, a willingness to engage with diverse perspectives, and the courage to confront our own biases and limitations.

Seeking truth also necessitates inner alignment – a state of congruence between our thoughts, emotions, and actions. It requires us to examine our own beliefs, values, and motivations, ensuring they align with the principles we hold dear. Inner alignment enables us to live authentically, fostering a deep sense of integrity and wholeness. When we align our actions with our inner truth, we cultivate a sense of inner peace and harmony.

In a world filled with noise and conflicting narratives, the importance of truth cannot be overstated. Truth serves as a compass that guides our decisions, actions, and interactions with others. It is the foundation upon which trust and meaningful relationships are built. When we embody truth in our words and deeds, we inspire trust, foster genuine connections, and create an environment where authenticity thrives.

Moreover, seeking truth is an act of empowerment and liberation. It frees us from the constraints of ignorance, prejudice, and falsehoods. As we unravel the layers of falsehood and embrace the truth, we reclaim our autonomy and personal agency. Truth empowers us to make informed choices, to challenge oppressive systems, and to strive for justice and equality.

The pursuit of truth is not without its challenges. It requires courage to confront uncomfortable realities, to question long-held beliefs, and to navigate through uncertainty. It demands resilience in the face of adversity, for the path of truth-seeking may be met with resistance and opposition. Yet, the rewards are profound – a deepened understanding of ourselves and the world, a heightened sense of purpose, and the ability to make a positive impact on the lives of others.

In conclusion, the concept of truth is a powerful force that invites us to embark on a transformative journey of seeking knowledge, understanding, and inner alignment. It is through this journey that we discover our authentic selves, forge meaningful connections with others, and contribute to the greater good. Let us embrace the pursuit of truth with open hearts and minds, knowing that it holds the key to unlocking our fullest potential and shaping a more enlightened and compassionate world.

CHAPTER 10

Living the Teachings: Applying the Seven Grandfathers in Daily Life

The teachings of the Seven Grandfathers hold profound wisdom and guidance for living a fulfilling and purposeful life. These teachings, rooted in the traditions of the Anishinaabe people, offer timeless principles that can be applied in our daily lives, fostering personal growth, harmony, and interconnectedness.

At the core of these teachings lies a call to embrace virtues that lead to balanced and compassionate living. Each of the Seven Grandfathers represents a virtue that, when cultivated and embodied, has the power to transform our thoughts, actions, and interactions with the world.

The first teaching, Love (Zaagidwin), invites us to cultivate a deep sense of compassion, empathy, and unity. By embracing love in our hearts, we open ourselves to understanding and valuing the interconnectedness of all beings. Love guides us to treat others with kindness, respect, and acceptance, fostering harmonious relationships and nurturing a sense of belonging.

The second teaching, Respect (Mnaadendmowin), emphasizes the importance of honoring oneself, others, and the natural world. Respect encourages us to recognize the inherent worth and dignity of every individual and to approach others with humility and consideration. By embodying respect, we create a space where diverse perspectives are valued, conflicts are resolved peacefully, and the natural world is cherished and protected.

The third teaching, Bravery (Aakode'ewin), calls us to embrace courage in the face of challenges. It empowers us to confront our fears, step out of our comfort zones, and pursue our dreams and aspirations. Bravery inspires us to take a stand for justice, advocate for change, and overcome obstacles on the path to personal and collective growth.

The fourth teaching, Honesty (Debwewin), encourages us to live in truth and authenticity. It invites us to be honest with ourselves and others, to speak our truth with integrity, and to act in alignment with our values. Honesty fosters trust, transparency, and genuine connections, creating an environment where authenticity and growth can flourish.

The fifth teaching, Humility (Dbe'ewin), teaches us to embrace humility as a source of strength. Humility reminds us of our interconnectedness with all beings and encourages us to approach life with a sense of openness, curiosity, and willingness to learn from others. It invites us to let go of ego-driven desires and to recognize that true wisdom comes from a place of humility.

The sixth teaching, Wisdom (Nibwaakaawin), emphasizes the importance of seeking knowledge, understanding, and inner alignment. Wisdom invites us to engage in lifelong learning, to listen to the wisdom of our ancestors, and to reflect on our experiences with discernment. It encourages us to integrate knowledge with intuition and to make wise choices that align with our values and purpose.

The seventh teaching, Truth (Debwewin), guides us to seek and embrace truth in all aspects of life. It urges us to question, explore, and uncover the deeper truths that resonate with our souls. Truth calls us to be honest with ourselves, to seek genuine understanding, and to align our thoughts, words, and actions with our inner truth.

To truly live the teachings of the Seven Grandfathers, we must embody these virtues in our daily lives. It is not enough to simply understand their concepts intellectually; we must practice them with intention and commitment. By applying the teachings in our thoughts, choices, and interactions, we cultivate a life of purpose, meaning, and contribution.

In our relationships, we can express love and respect, honoring the dignity and worth of others. We can embrace bravery to pursue our passions and make a positive impact on the world. We can uphold honesty, fostering trust and authenticity in our communication. We can embrace humility, recognizing the wisdom in others and valuing diverse perspectives.

CHAPTER 11

The Power of Anishinaabe Ceremony and Rituals

The Anishinaabe people have a deep reverence for ceremony and rituals, recognizing their power to connect with the spiritual realm, honor ancestors, and maintain harmony within the natural world. These sacred practices are an integral part of the Anishinaabe culture, carrying wisdom, healing, and transformational energy. The power of Anishinaabe ceremony and rituals extends beyond individual experiences, weaving a collective tapestry of community, identity, and spiritual connection.

Ceremony holds a central place in Anishinaabe life, providing a sacred space for individuals to commune with the Great Spirit, express gratitude, seek guidance, and restore balance. The ritualistic nature of ceremonies serves as a bridge between the physical and spiritual realms, fostering a deep sense of interconnectedness and oneness with the universe.

Sweat Lodge ceremonies, also known as Inipi, are revered for their purification and spiritual renewal properties. Participants enter a domed structure, heated with hot stones, to engage in prayer, reflection, and cleansing. The intense heat, darkness, and rhythmic chanting create a transformative environment that purifies the mind, body, and spirit. Through this ceremony, individuals shed negativity, release emotional burdens, and emerge with a renewed sense of clarity, strength, and purpose.

The Pipe Ceremony, or Wiigwaasabakoon, is a sacred ritual that involves the smoking of a ceremonial pipe. This act symbolizes unity, reverence, and the connection between the earthly and spiritual realms. Participants pass the pipe, offering prayers and tobacco as a sign of respect and gratitude. The Pipe Ceremony is a time-honored tradition that deepens spiritual connection, fosters community harmony, and invokes guidance from ancestors and spirits.

Sun Dance, or Bimizi Giizis, is a powerful ceremony that celebrates renewal, sacrifice, and spiritual growth. Participants undertake a physical and mental journey through fasting, prayer, and dance. The dance, performed in a circular formation, signifies the eternal cycle of life and the interconnectedness of all beings. Sun Dance is a profound ritual that invokes spiritual guidance, honors ancestral traditions, and fosters personal transformation.

Vision Quest, or Misko Minjimendan, is a sacred rite of passage that involves solitary reflection and communion with nature. Participants venture into the wilderness, seeking spiritual guidance, purpose, and personal revelation. Through fasting, meditation, and prayer, individuals open themselves to the wisdom of the natural world and the whispers of the Great Spirit. Vision Quests offer profound insights, clarity, and a deepening of spiritual connection.

These are just a few examples of the diverse ceremonies and rituals within the Anishinaabe tradition. Each ceremony holds its unique significance and purpose, inviting individuals to connect with their ancestral roots, deepen their spirituality, and find solace in the wisdom of their elders.

The power of Anishinaabe ceremony and rituals lies in their ability to transcend time and space, bridging the past, present, and future. They provide a pathway to healing, self-discovery, and cultural revitalization. Through these sacred practices, individuals not only connect with their own heritage but also contribute to the collective healing and well-being of their communities.

In a world where disconnection, stress, and fragmentation often prevail, the power of Anishinaabe ceremony and rituals reminds us of the importance of spiritual grounding, cultural preservation, and honoring the interconnectedness of all beings. As we open ourselves to the teachings and practices of the Anishinaabe people, we embrace a profound opportunity to rediscover our own spiritual essence, cultivate harmony, and walk the path of balance and respect in harmony with the natural world.

CHAPTER 12

Healing and Transformation: The Journey to Wholeness

In the depths of our souls, a powerful longing resides—a yearning to heal, transform, and discover the profound essence of our being. The journey to wholeness beckons us, inviting us to embark on a path of self-discovery, resilience, and profound transformation. It is a journey that calls upon our deepest emotions, urging us to confront our fears, mend our wounds, and awaken the dormant potential within us.

As we heed the call for healing, we embrace the understanding that it is not merely the absence of pain but a holistic process that encompasses our physical, emotional, and spiritual well-being. It is a sacred journey that demands our utmost courage, vulnerability, and commitment.

At the heart of this journey lies the recognition of self-compassion and self-love. We learn to embrace ourselves with tenderness and understanding, acknowledging our vulnerabilities and nurturing our inner child. Through self-compassion, we create a safe space within us—a sanctuary where healing can take root and bloom.

To embark on the path of healing, we must be willing to release the emotional baggage and trauma that burden our souls. It is a courageous act of facing our past, confronting our deepest fears, and allowing the wounds to heal. Through forgiveness, both towards ourselves and others, we liberate ourselves from the shackles of resentment and pain, creating space for profound transformation and inner peace.

Spirituality becomes an unwavering companion on our journey—a guiding light that illuminates our path. As we connect with our spirituality, we tap into a wellspring of wisdom and guidance. Through meditation, prayer, or sacred rituals, we immerse ourselves in the divine energy that surrounds us, allowing it to infuse our being with healing vibrations.

Embracing our authenticity is an essential step towards wholeness. It is a profound act of honoring our true selves, aligning with our passions, and living in alignment with our values. By shedding the masks we wear and embracing our uniqueness, we unlock the dormant potential within us, igniting the flame of purpose and meaning.

The mind-body connection serves as a powerful conduit for healing and transformation. By nurturing this connection through practices such as yoga, mindfulness, and holistic wellness, we cultivate harmony within ourselves. We become attuned to the needs of our bodies, minds, and spirits, facilitating deep healing and integration.

As we embark on this transformative journey, relationships take on a new significance. We recognize the importance of cultivating healthy connections, setting boundaries, and fostering authentic communication. Surrounding ourselves with supportive and loving individuals creates a nurturing environment that fuels our growth and enhances our well-being.

Ultimately, the journey to wholeness is a lifelong endeavor. It requires us to embrace the ebb and flow of life, to remain open to the lessons presented to us, and to continually evolve and expand. As we embrace our own healing and transformation, we become beacons of light, inspiring others to embark on their own paths of self-discovery and wholeness.

Examining how the Seven Generations and Seven Grandfathers Teachings can Support Personal Healing, Growth, and Transformation.

In the depths of our souls, there exists a profound longing for healing, growth, and transformation. We yearn to uncover the secrets that will guide us towards a life of wholeness and purpose. It is in this quest that we discover the timeless wisdom embedded within the teachings of the Seven Generations and Seven Grandfathers—a wisdom that holds the key to unlocking our true potential and igniting the flame of profound transformation.

The teachings of the Seven Generations remind us of our interconnectedness—the realization that our actions ripple through time, impacting not only our present but also the lives of future generations. We are called to pause and reflect on the choices we make, for they have the power to shape the world that our children and grandchildren will inherit.

At the heart of these teachings lies love—love that transcends boundaries, love that unites us as a human family. Love becomes our guiding light, illuminating the path towards healing and growth. It compels us to treat one another with kindness, empathy, and respect, fostering a nurturing environment where personal transformation can flourish.

As we delve deeper into the teachings, we encounter the virtue of wisdom—a timeless guide that leads us towards understanding, discernment, and inner alignment. Through seeking knowledge and embracing a lifelong journey of learning, we expand our minds, open our hearts, and uncover the profound truths that lie within us. It is through wisdom that we find the courage to confront our shadows, embrace our strengths, and embark on a journey of self-discovery.

The teachings also emphasize the importance of respect—for ourselves, for others, and for the natural world that sustains us. When we approach life with reverence and gratitude, we foster a deep sense of connection and harmony. Respect becomes the foundation upon which personal healing and growth can take root, allowing us to honor our own journey, embrace the diversity of others, and recognize the inherent value in all living beings.

Bravery becomes our ally as we navigate the turbulent waters of personal transformation. It is the courage to face our fears, to step outside our comfort zones, and to embrace the unknown. Through acts of bravery, we dismantle the walls of self-doubt and limitation, propelling ourselves towards new horizons of growth and possibility.

Honesty guides us along this transformative path, encouraging us to live authentically and in truth. When we embrace honesty, we shed the layers of masks and facades, revealing our true selves to the world. Honesty becomes a catalyst for personal healing, as we release the burdens of pretense and embrace the freedom that comes from living in alignment with our core values.

Humility serves as a powerful anchor on our journey—a reminder that we are part of something greater than ourselves. It is through humility that we recognize the interconnectedness of all beings and surrender the need for control. In this surrender, we open ourselves to the flow of life, allowing the currents of growth and transformation to carry us towards our highest potential.

Truth becomes our guiding star—a compass that directs our actions and choices. By seeking truth in all aspects of life, we align ourselves with our deepest purpose and values. Truth becomes the foundation upon which personal healing, growth, and transformation can thrive.

As we embrace the profound teachings of the Seven Generations and Seven Grandfathers, we embark on a sacred journey—a journey that leads us towards personal healing, growth, and transformation. It is a journey that requires courage, vulnerability, and a willingness to confront our own shadows. But in this journey, we discover the immense power within us—the power to heal, to grow, and to transform.

So, dear seeker of personal transformation, I invite you to immerse yourself in the wisdom of the Seven Generations and Seven Grandfathers teachings. Embrace the interconnectedness of all beings, cultivate love, wisdom, respect, bravery, honesty, humility, and truth within your being. In doing so, you will unlock the transformative power that lies dormant within you, and embark on a journey of profound healing, growth, and transformation—a journey that will not only uplift your own life but also ripple outwards, touching the lives of generations to come.

CHAPTER 13

The Seven Generations in a Modern World: Applying the Teachings to Global Challenges

In our fast-paced, interconnected world, we find ourselves grappling with unprecedented global challenges that require collective action and a fresh approach. It is within this context that the teachings of the Seven Generations and Seven Grandfathers hold profound significance. These ancient teachings, rooted in the wisdom of the Anishinaabe people, offer a timeless guide for navigating the complexities of our modern era and addressing pressing global issues.

At the core of these teachings lies the recognition of our interconnectedness with all beings and the natural world. This foundational belief serves as a guiding principle for understanding our responsibilities to future generations and the planet. By embracing this interconnectedness, we can foster a sense of global citizenship, where the well-being of all is intricately linked to our own.

Love, one of the virtues emphasized in the teachings, becomes a transformative force in our pursuit of solutions to global challenges. Love teaches us compassion, empathy, and the power of unity. By embodying love in our actions, we can bridge divides, break down barriers, and work towards a world where everyone is valued and supported.

Wisdom, another crucial virtue, guides us in making informed decisions that consider the long-term impacts on both people and the planet. In an era of rapid change and information overload, the teachings of the Seven Generations remind us to seek wisdom from within, drawing on ancestral knowledge and our collective experiences to navigate the complexities of our modern world.

Respect, both for ourselves and others, is a cornerstone of the teachings. By cultivating respect, we can foster harmonious relationships, honor diverse perspectives, and foster inclusivity. Respect also extends to the natural world, reminding us of our duty to protect and preserve the delicate balance of our ecosystems for future generations.

As we confront global challenges, we must summon the bravery to face adversity and take courageous action. The teachings encourage us to challenge the status quo, speak truth to power, and advocate for justice. By embracing bravery, we can dismantle oppressive systems, fight for human rights, and create a more equitable world.

Honesty and transparency are essential in our efforts to address global challenges. The teachings call us to live authentically, to be accountable for our actions, and to demand transparency from those in positions of power. By upholding honesty and accountability, we can cultivate trust and integrity, creating a foundation for positive change.

Humility reminds us of our place in the world and the importance of collaboration. In a world often driven by ego and self-interest, humility calls us to recognize the value of diverse perspectives, to listen with an open heart, and to work together to find collective solutions. Through humility, we can build bridges, foster understanding, and nurture a culture of collaboration.

The pursuit of truth and justice is paramount in addressing global challenges. The teachings guide us to seek truth, challenge falsehoods, and advocate for justice for all people. By embracing the pursuit of truth and justice, we can create a world where equality, fairness, and the inherent dignity of every individual are upheld.

In conclusion, the teachings of the Seven Generations and Seven Grandfathers offer profound guidance for addressing global challenges in our modern era. By embracing the virtues of interconnectedness, love, wisdom, respect, bravery, honesty, humility, and truth, we can pave the way for a more sustainable, just, and compassionate world. Let us heed the wisdom of the Anishinaabe teachings and embark on a collective journey towards a brighter future for all.

CHAPTER 13

Walking the Path of the Seven Generations: Inspiring Stories of Transformation

Lost Stories of the Anishinaabe Culture.

<u>**Aiyana Nokomis**</u> (Aiyana - Eternal Blossom)

Once upon a time in a small village nestled deep within the lush forests of a land rich in ancestral wisdom, there lived a young woman named Aiyana. Aiyana had always felt a deep connection to nature and a yearning to understand the deeper meaning of life. Little did she know that her path would lead her to the profound teachings of the Seven Grandfathers.

Aiyana grew up in a community that cherished its cultural heritage and held the values of respect, love, and wisdom in high regard. However, like many young people of her generation, she found herself navigating the complexities of the modern world, where materialism and individualism often overshadowed the deeper spiritual essence of life.

One day, while exploring the village library, Aiyana stumbled upon an ancient book that spoke of the sacred teachings of the Seven Grandfathers. Intrigued by the wisdom it promised, she immersed herself in its pages, eager to discover the transformative power within.

As she delved deeper into the teachings, Aiyana began to realize the profound impact they could have on her life and the world around her. The teachings reminded her of the importance of embracing love, respect, bravery, honesty, humility, truth, and wisdom in all aspects of life.

Inspired by these teachings, Aiyana embarked on a personal journey of self-discovery and transformation. She began by cultivating love within herself, nurturing self-compassion and kindness. She practiced acts of kindness towards others, realizing that even the smallest gestures of love could create ripples of positivity in the world.

With newfound respect for herself, others, and the natural world, Aiyana became an advocate for environmental stewardship. She rallied her community to take action, organizing tree-planting initiatives, and educating others on sustainable living practices. Through her efforts, the village became a beacon of environmental consciousness, inspiring neighboring communities to follow suit.

Aiyana's path was not without challenges. At times, fear and doubt would creep into her mind, but she remembered the teachings of bravery and courage. With unwavering determination, she faced her fears head-on, challenging societal norms and advocating for social justice. Her actions inspired others to rise above their fears, leading to a more inclusive and equitable society.

Throughout her journey, Aiyana remained committed to living in truth and authenticity. She recognized the power of honest communication, both with herself and others, fostering deep and meaningful connections. Her willingness to be vulnerable allowed others to do the same, creating a community built on trust and openness.

As Aiyana continued to embody the teachings, she realized that her transformation was not limited to her own life. The positive changes she experienced began to ripple outward, touching the lives of those around her. Through her example, others began to awaken to their own potential and the immense power of the Seven Grandfathers' teachings.

Years passed, and Aiyana became a revered elder in her community, guiding younger generations on their own journeys of self-discovery. Her wisdom and compassionate leadership served as a beacon of hope and inspiration, reminding everyone of the profound impact that embracing the teachings could have on their lives and the world.

Aiyana's story serves as a testament to the transformative power of the Seven Grandfathers' teachings. It reminds us that by embodying love, respect, bravery, honesty, humility, truth, and wisdom, we have the ability to create profound and lasting change in ourselves and our communities. May we all walk the path of the Seven Grandfathers and witness the profound transformations that lie within.

Nodin(Nodin - Wind) (Last Name Unknown)

Once upon a time, in a small Anishinaabe community nestled by the shores of a pristine lake, there lived a young woman named Nodin (meaning "wind" in Anishinaabe). Nodin was known for her vibrant spirit and her deep connection to nature. From a young age, she felt a strong pull to explore the teachings of the Seven Grandfathers and embark on a journey of self-discovery.

Nodin's journey began when she met an elder named Makwa (meaning "bear" in Anishinaabe), a wise and gentle soul who possessed a wealth of ancestral knowledge. Intrigued by Nodin's eagerness to learn, Makwa took her under his wing and became her mentor.

Under Makwa's guidance, Nodin embarked on a series of spiritual quests, immersing herself in the ancient rituals and ceremonies of her people. She fasted in the wilderness, seeking a deeper connection to the natural world and the spiritual realm. She listened to the whispers of the wind and observed the dance of the stars, learning to read the signs and messages that the universe presented to her.

Through her experiences, Nodin discovered the power of Miigwetch (meaning "gratitude" in Anishinaabe) and the practice of acknowledging and appreciating the blessings in her life. She learned that gratitude opened the door to abundance and invited positive energy into her existence.

As Nodin delved deeper into the teachings, she embraced the value of Zaagidwin (meaning "love" in Anishinaabe). She learned that love was not merely a fleeting emotion, but a force that transcended boundaries and connected all living beings. Nodin practiced compassion and kindness, lending a helping hand to those in need and fostering unity within her community.

Nodin's transformative journey also led her to explore the virtues of Mnaadendmowin (meaning "respect" in Anishinaabe) and Aakode'ewin (meaning "bravery" in Anishinaabe). She recognized the importance of honoring herself, others, and the natural world, treating each with reverence and dignity. She also found the courage to face her fears, stepping outside her comfort zone to embrace new challenges and opportunities for growth.

Through her devotion to the Seven Grandfathers' teachings, Nodin became a beacon of light within her community. Her presence radiated wisdom, love, and humility, inspiring others to embark on their own journeys of self-discovery and transformation.

As years passed, Nodin's influence spread far beyond her small community. People from different walks of life were drawn to her, seeking guidance and solace in their own struggles. She became a storyteller, sharing the ancient wisdom of the Anishinaabe people and helping others find their own paths to healing and fulfillment.

Nodin's journey of self-discovery and transformation serves as a reminder that the teachings of the Seven Grandfathers are timeless and universal. They hold the power to shape our lives, guide our actions, and foster a harmonious connection with ourselves, others, and the world around us.

May we all embark on our own sacred journeys, embracing the teachings of the Seven Grandfathers and walking the path of self-discovery, healing, and transformation. Miigwetch.

Nokomis(Grandmother - A sacred term in Anishinaabe culture)

Once upon a time, in a small Anishinaabe community nestled along the shores of a crystal-clear lake, there lived a young woman named Nokomis. Nokomis had always felt a deep connection to the land and the sacred waters that surrounded her village. She had heard stories from her elders about the profound wisdom and healing powers contained within these waters.

One day, Nokomis embarked on a spiritual journey to discover the secrets of the sacred waters. She sought guidance from the village elders, who shared ancient teachings about the interconnectedness of all life and the importance of honoring and protecting the natural world.

With a heart full of reverence, Nokomis set off on a canoe, following the river that led her to the heart of the wilderness. Along her journey, she encountered various challenges and learned valuable lessons about resilience, patience, and trust in the guidance of the Creator.

As she paddled deeper into the wilderness, Nokomis noticed a significant change within herself. She began to develop a heightened sense of awareness and a profound connection to the spirits of the land and water. She could feel the pulsating energy of the Earth beneath her fingertips and hear the whispers of the ancestors carried by the wind.

During her solitary nights by the campfire, Nokomis would share stories with the stars, pouring her heart out and seeking guidance. In these quiet moments, she realized that the sacred waters held not only physical healing properties but also the power to cleanse and rejuvenate one's spirit.

One moonlit night, as Nokomis was gazing at her reflection in the still waters of a serene lake, she felt a surge of energy wash over her. It was as if the ancestors were speaking to her, guiding her to use her newfound knowledge and connection to help heal her community and the world beyond.

Through her experiences, Nokomis embodies and demonstrates the virtues and principles that are central to the Seven Grandfathers teachings.

Nokomis's journey reflects the principle of Nibwaakaawin (Wisdom), as she seeks guidance from her village elders and embarks on a spiritual quest to gain deeper understanding and connection with the sacred waters. Her encounters and challenges along the way contribute to her growth and the accumulation of wisdom.

Nokomis's reverence for the natural world and her commitment to protect and honor the sacred waters demonstrate the virtue of Mnaadendmowin (Respect). She recognizes the interconnectedness of all beings and understands the importance of maintaining balance and harmony with nature.

As Nokomis overcomes obstacles and develops resilience and patience, she exemplifies the virtue of Aakode'ewin (Bravery). Her willingness to venture into the unknown, face her fears, and trust in the guidance of the Creator showcases her bravery and determination.

Throughout her journey, Nokomis learns to listen to her inner voice and connect with the spirits of the land and water. This embodies the virtue of Zaagidwin (Love), as she cultivates compassion and unity with the natural world, recognizing the inherent value and interconnectedness of all beings.

Nokomis's commitment to sharing her wisdom and teachings with her community reflects the virtue of Debwewin (Truth). She imparts the knowledge she has gained from her journey, encouraging others to honor and protect the sacred waters and guiding them towards a deeper understanding of their responsibility as caretakers of the land.

Finally, Nokomis's humility and recognition of her role as a steward of the land align with the virtue of Gwekwaadiziwin (Honesty). She acknowledges her connection to the sacred waters and uses her knowledge to inspire and educate others, humbly embracing her role as a catalyst for change.

In this way, the story of Nokomis encompasses the essence of the Seven Grandfathers teachings, showcasing the transformative power of living in alignment with these virtues and principles.

Returning to her village, Nokomis shared the teachings she had learned on her journey. She organised ceremonies of gratitude and offerings to the sacred waters, encouraging her people to honor and protect these precious resources. She spoke of the interconnectedness of all beings and the need for balance and harmony in our relationship with the natural world.

Nokomis became a beacon of inspiration for her community, guiding them towards a deeper understanding of their responsibility as stewards of the land and water. She encouraged sustainable practices, such as traditional harvesting and conservation efforts, ensuring that future generations would inherit a thriving and bountiful environment.

The legacy of Nokomis lived on, as her teachings spread beyond her village, reaching neighboring communities and inspiring others to reconnect with their ancestral wisdom. Her journey of self-discovery and connection to the sacred waters became a symbol of hope and renewal for all who heard her story.

And so, the spirit of Nokomis continues to guide generations, reminding them of the power that lies within the sacred waters and the profound impact

that can be made when one listens to the whispers
of the land and follows the path of the heart

Conclusion

Embracing the Teachings and Leaving a Lasting Legacy

In the depths of our existence lies a timeless wisdom, passed down through generations, that beckons us to embrace profound teachings and leave behind a lasting legacy. Rooted in the Anishinaabe culture, the Seven Generations and Seven Grandfathers teachings illuminate a path of wisdom, compassion, and interconnectedness. As we immerse ourselves in these sacred teachings, we discover the transformative power they hold in shaping our lives and the world around us.

At the core of the Seven Generations teachings is the understanding that our actions today ripple through time, impacting not only our immediate reality but also the lives of those who will come after us. This awareness calls us to step into our roles as caretakers of the Earth and stewards of future generations. By embodying the principles of love, respect, bravery, honesty, humility, truth, and wisdom, we become catalysts for positive change.

When we embrace these teachings, we embark on a journey of personal and collective transformation. Love becomes the driving force behind our interactions, fostering compassion, understanding, and unity. We learn to respect ourselves, others, and the natural world, recognizing the inherent value and interconnectedness of all beings. Bravery empowers us to confront challenges and overcome adversity, while honesty guides us to live in truth and authenticity. Humility becomes a source of strength, enabling us to learn from others and acknowledge our interconnectedness. Truth becomes our compass, guiding our thoughts, choices, and interactions with integrity and alignment. And wisdom illuminates our path, leading us towards a purposeful and fulfilling life.

As we navigate this transformative journey, we find ourselves called to leave a lasting legacy. It is not merely about the accumulation of material possessions or worldly achievements, but rather about the impact we have on the lives of others and the world we inhabit. Through our actions, we have the power to inspire, uplift, and empower future generations. By embodying the teachings and living in alignment with them, we create a ripple effect that extends far beyond our own existence.

Imagine a world where the wisdom of the Seven Generations and Seven Grandfathers teachings permeates every aspect of society. It is a world where love, respect, bravery, honesty, humility, truth, and wisdom are the guiding principles in all human interactions. In this world, individuals are empowered to embrace their unique gifts and talents, fostering a collective harmony that transcends cultural, social, and geographical boundaries. Through our legacy of love and wisdom, we pave the way for a brighter future, a world where the interconnectedness of all beings is cherished and celebrated.

In conclusion, embracing the teachings of the Seven Generations and Seven Grandfathers is a transformative journey of personal growth and collective healing. It is a call to embody the virtues that have guided our ancestors for centuries, and to leave a lasting legacy of love, wisdom, and interconnectedness. As we navigate the path, let us remember that our actions today have the power to shape the world for generations to come. May we embrace the teachings, walk in harmony with the Earth, and sow the seeds of a future rooted in love and compassion. Together, let us create a legacy that transcends time and leaves an indelible mark on the tapestry of humanity.

Author's Note

For taking the time to read this book, I can only say Miigwetch! This will actually be my first book since my degree. I was ecstatic while writing this and it's a real pleasure to put knowledge about this amazing culture out there for more people to learn about. I hope to write more books like this in the future.

Please consider leaving me an honest review as it'll help me know where my mistakes are in this book and where to improve in my next book.

Once again, Miigwetch :)

www.ingramcontent.com/pod-product-compliance
Lightning Source LLC
Chambersburg PA
CBHW060845220526
45466CB00003B/1250